Layers of Learning

Year One • Unit Three

Ancient Europe
Global Grids
Earth & Moon
Crafts

HooDoo Publishing
United States of America
©2014 Layers of Learning
Copies of maps or activities may be made for a particular family or classroom.
ISBN 978-1494409456

If you wish to reproduce or print excerpts of this publication, please contact us at contact@layers-of-learning.com for permission. Thank you for respecting copyright laws.

Units At A Glance: Topics For All Four Years of the Layers of Learning Program

1	History	Geography	Science	The Arts
1	Mesopotamia	Maps & Globes	Planets	Cave Paintings
2	Egypt	Map Keys	Stars	Egyptian Art
3	Europe	Global Grids	Earth & Moon	Crafts
4	Ancient Greece	Wonders	Satellites	Greek Art
5	Babylon	Mapping People	Humans in Space	Poetry
6	The Levant	Physical Earth	Laws of Motion	List Poems
7	Phoenicians	Oceans	Motion	Moral Stories
8	Assyrians	Deserts	Fluids	Rhythm
9	Persians	Arctic	Waves	Melody
10	Ancient China	Forests	Machines	Chinese Art
11	Early Japan	Mountains	States of Matter	Line & Shape
12	Arabia	Rivers & Lakes	Atoms	Color & Value
13	Ancient India	Grasslands	Elements	Texture & Form
14	Ancient Africa	Africa	Bonding	African Tales
15	First North Americans	North America	Salts	Creative Kids
16	Ancient South America	South America	Plants	South American Art
17	Celts	Europe	Flowering Plants	Jewelry
18	Roman Republic	Asia	Trees	Roman Art
19	Christianity	Australia & Oceania	Simple Plants	Instruments
20	Roman Empire	You Explore	Fungi	Composing Music

2	History	Geography	Science	The Arts
1	Byzantines	Turkey	Climate & Seasons	Byzantine Art
2	Barbarians	Ireland	Forecasting	Illumination
3	Islam	Arabian Peninsula	Clouds & Precipitation	Creative Kids
4	Vikings	Norway	Special Effects	Viking Art
5	Anglo Saxons	Britain	Wild Weather	King Arthur Tales
6	Charlemagne	France	Cells and DNA	Carolingian Art
7	Normans	Nigeria	Skeletons	Canterbury Tales
8	Feudal System	Germany	Muscles, Skin, & Cardiopulmonary	Gothic Art
9	Crusades	Balkans	Digestive & Senses	Religious Art
10	Burgundy, Venice, Spain	Switzerland	Nerves	Oil Paints
11	Wars of the Roses	Russia	Health	Minstrels & Plays
12	Eastern Europe	Hungary	Metals	Printmaking
13	African Kingdoms	Mali	Carbon Chem	Textiles
14	Asian Kingdoms	Southeast Asia	Non-metals	Vivid Language
15	Mongols	Caucasus	Gases	Fun With Poetry
16	Medieval China & Japan	China	Electricity	Asian Arts
17	Pacific Peoples	Micronesia	Circuits	Arts of the Islands
18	American Peoples	Canada	Technology	Indian Legends
19	The Renaissance	Italy	Magnetism	Renaissance Art I
20	Explorers	Caribbean Sea	Motors	Renaissance Art II

3	History	Geography	Science	The Arts
1	Age of Exploration	Argentina and Chile	Classification & Insects	Fairy Tales
2	The Ottoman Empire	Egypt and Libya	Reptiles & Amphibians	Poetry
3	Mogul Empire	Pakistan & Afghanistan	Fish	Mogul Arts
4	Reformation	Angola & Zambia	Birds	Reformation Art
5	Renaissance England	Tanzania & Kenya	Mammals & Primates	Shakespeare
6	Thirty Years' War	Spain	Sound	Baroque Music
7	The Dutch	Netherlands	Light & Optics	Baroque Art I
8	France	Indonesia	Bending Light	Baroque Art II
9	The Enlightenment	Korean Pen.	Color	Art Journaling
10	Russia & Prussia	Central Asia	History of Science	Watercolors
11	Conquistadors	Baltic States	Igneous Rocks	Creative Kids
12	Settlers	Peru & Bolivia	Sedimentary Rocks	Native American Art
13	13 Colonies	Central America	Metamorphic Rocks	Settler Sayings
14	Slave Trade	Brazil	Gems & Minerals	Colonial Art
15	The South Pacific	Australasia	Fossils	Principles of Art
16	The British in India	India	Chemical Reactions	Classical Music
17	Boston Tea Party	Japan	Reversible Reactions	Folk Music
18	Founding Fathers	Iran	Compounds & Solutions	Rococo
19	Declaring Independence	Samoa and Tonga	Oxidation & Reduction	Creative Crafts I
20	The American Revolution	South Africa	Acids & Bases	Creative Crafts II

4	History	Geography	Science	The Arts
1	American Government	USA	Heat & Temperature	Patriotic Music
2	Expanding Nation	Pacific States	Motors & Engines	Tall Tales
3	Industrial Revolution	U.S. Landscapes	Energy	Romantic Art I
4	Revolutions	Mountain West States	Energy Sources	Romantic Art II
5	Africa	U.S. Political Maps	Energy Conversion	Impressionism I
6	The West	Southwest States	Earth Structure	Impressionism II
7	Civil War	National Parks	Plate Tectonics	Post-Impressionism
8	World War I	Plains States	Earthquakes	Expressionism
9	Totalitarianism	U.S. Economics	Volcanoes	Abstract Art
10	Great Depression	Heartland States	Mountain Building	Kinds of Art
11	World War II	Symbols and Landmarks	Chemistry of Air & Water	War Art
12	Modern East Asia	The South States	Food Chemistry	Modern Art
13	India's Independence	People of America	Industry	Pop Art
14	Israel	Appalachian States	Chemistry of Farming	Modern Music
15	Cold War	U.S. Territories	Chemistry of Medicine	Free Verse
16	Vietnam War	Atlantic States	Food Chains	Photography
17	Latin America	New England States	Animal Groups	Latin American Art
18	Civil Rights	Home State Study	Instincts	Theater & Film
19	Technology	Home State Study II	Habitats	Architecture
20	Terrorism	America in Review	Conservation	Creative Kids

This unit includes printables at the end. To make life easier for you we also created digital printable packs for each unit. To retrieve your printable pack for Unit 1-3, please visit

www.layers-of-learning.com/digital-printable-packs/

Put the printable pack in your shopping cart and use this coupon code:

1206UNIT1-3

Your printable pack will be free.

LAYERS OF LEARNING INTRODUCTION

This is part of a series of units in the Layers of Learning homeschool curriculum, including the subjects of history, geography, science, and the arts. Children from 1st through 12th can participate in the same curriculum at the same time - family school style.

The units are intended to be used in order as the basis of a complete curriculum (once you add in a systematic math, reading, and writing program). You begin with Year 1 Unit 1 no matter what ages your children are. Spend about 2 weeks on each unit. You pick and choose the activities within the unit that appeal to you and read the books from the book list that are available to you or find others on the same topic from your library. We highly recommend that you use the timeline in every history section as the backbone. Then flesh out your learning with reading and activities that highlight the topics you think are the most important.

Alternatively, you can use the units as activity ideas to supplement another curriculum in any order you wish. You can still use them with all ages of children at the same time.

When you've finished with Year One, move on to Year Two, Year Three, and Year Four. Then begin again with Year One and work your way through the years again. Now your children will be older, reading more involved books, and writing more in depth. When you have completed the sequence for the second time, you start again on it for the third and final time. If your student began with Layers of Learning in 1st grade and stayed with it all the way through she would go through the four year rotation three times, firmly cementing the information in her mind in ever increasing depth. At each level you should expect increasing amounts of outside reading and writing. High schoolers in particular should be reading extensively, and if possible, participating in discussion groups.

☺ ☺ ☺ These icons will guide you in spotting activities and books that are appropriate for the age of child you are working with. But if you think an activity is too juvenile or too difficult for your kids, adjust accordingly. The icons are not there as rules, just guides.

☺ GRADES 1-4
☺ GRADES 5-8
☺ GRADES 9-12

Within each unit we share:
- EXPLORATIONS, activities relating to the topic;
- EXPERIMENTS, usually associated with science topics;
- EXPEDITIONS, field trips;
- EXPLANATIONS, teacher helps or educational philosophies.

In the sidebars we also include Additional Layers, Famous Folks, Fabulous Facts, On the Web, and other extra related topics that can take you off on tangents, exploring the world and your interests with a bit more freedom. The curriculum will always be there to pull you back on track when you're ready.

You can learn more about how to use this curriculum at www.layers-of-learning.com/layers-of-learning-program/

ANCIENT EUROPE – GLOBAL GRIDS – EARTH & MOON – CRAFTS

UNIT THREE
ANCIENT EUROPE – GLOBAL GRIDS – EARTH & MOON – CRAFTS

It is important that students bring a certain ragamuffin, barefoot irreverence to their studies; they are not here to worship what is known, but to question it.
-Jacob Bronowski

	LIBRARY LIST:
HISTORY	Search for: ancient Europe, ancient Britons, megalithic Europe, Europe-history, Stonehenge. A hard to find subject, check encyclopedias for information. ☺ ☺ ☺ The Story of Stonehenge and Other Megalithic Sites by A.G. Smith. From Dover: a coloring book with detailed captions. ☺ ☺ Ice Mummy by Mark Dubowski. A level 4 easy reader from DK about the 5000 year old mummy found in ice. ☺ ☺ ☺ Build Your Own Stonehenge from Running Press Kits. A model Stonehenge to assemble for all ages. ☺ If Stones Could Speak: Unlocking the Secrets of Stonehenge by Marc Aronson and Mike Pearson. From National Geographic Kids. ☺ ☺ Frozen Man by David Getz. All about the discovery of a 5000 year old body found in a glacier in Italy. ☺ ☺ Bodies From the Bog by James M. Deen. About the well preserved finds of ancient bodies and what we learned about them. ☺ ☺ Lost Treasures of the Ancient World: Stonehenge and the Ancient Britons: movie
GEOGRAPHY	Search for: latitude and longitude, navigation ☺ Latitude and Longitude by Rebecca Augberg. For young beginners. ☺ Tools of Navigation: A Kids Guide to the History and Science of Finding Your Way by Rachel Dickinson. How have people found their way in and out of unexplored places on Earth? ☺ ☺ Latitude and Longitude and How To Find Them by W.J. Miller. A classic brought back into print. This is a mathematically oriented book for the older student. Can be downloaded for free from Forgotten Books.

Ancient Europe – Global Grids – Earth & Moon – Crafts

Science

Search for: earth, planet earth, moon

🙂 <u>You're Aboard Spaceship Earth</u> by Patricia Lauber. Earth is the perfect ship to ride through space; find out why.

🙂 <u>Where Does the Moon Go?</u> By Sidney Rosen. A good overall description of the moon, its properties, and phases for young children.

🙂 <u>Sun, Moon and Stars</u> by Stephanie Turnbull. An easy reader for young children.

🙂 <u>Our Wonderful Earth</u> by Nicola Baxter.

🙂 <u>On Earth</u> by G. Brian Karas. Excellent description of Earth's phases, seasons, and cycles.

🙂 🙂 🙂 <u>Blue Planet</u> IMAX movie directed by Ben Burtt. Amazing pictures of earth from space.

🙂 🙂 🙂 <u>The Wonders of God's Creation: Planet Earth</u> movie from Moody video. Often sold as part of a three volume set, tells the Christian/Creationist view of the earth.

🙂 <u>Don't Know Much About the Planet Earth</u> by Kenneth C. Davis. Fascinating facts about the earth for middle grades.

🙂 <u>E-guides: Earth</u> by Matt Turner. From DK; covers formation of the earth through structure of the earth and is internet linked with its own website.

🙂 🙂 <u>Earth</u> edited by James F. Luhr. From DK; filled with photos and captions plus plenty of text, and covers formation of the earth, cycles and seasons, oceans and land, and the structure of the earth.

🙂 🙂 <u>The Moon</u> by Isaac Asimov.

🙂 <u>Harmonies of the World</u> by Johannes Kepler.

The Arts

Search for: craft projects, home decorating, woodworking, sewing, web design, weaving, knitting, garden crafts, clay, ceramics, quilting, etc. The internet is also a great source of information for project ideas on this subject.

🙂 🙂 🙂 <u>Kids Create: Art & Craft Ideas For 3 to 9 year-olds</u> by Laurie Carlson. Perfect for this unit, but great fun for anytime. Includes sculpting, paper crafts, printmaking, and more.

🙂 🙂 🙂 <u>Making Crafts From Your Kids Art</u> by Valerie Van Arsdale Schrader. Use kids' drawings to decorate everyday household items like tea cups, clocks, pillows, wrapping paper and more.

🙂 🙂 🙂 <u>Friendship Bracelets</u> by Laura Torres. From Klutz, this book comes with the embroidery floss and other supplies you need to make the bracelets. Perfect for your girls.

🙂 🙂 <u>Nature Crafts For Kids</u> by Gwen Diehn. More advanced crafts for kids nine and up. These projects will require adult help, but they are useful things you will keep around for years, not slapped together paper crafts you can't wait to toss.

🙂 <u>Leathercraft</u> by Linda Sue Eastman. Easy projects that will totally appeal to kids, everything from making a wallet to making a case for your hand-held video game. Requires that you purchase a few simple tools and the leather.

🙂 🙂 <u>Mark Kistler's Web Wizards</u> by Mark Kistler and Denis Dawson. For middle grades and up. Written to kids, explains and explores HTML, programming and adding awesome design elements to a web page.

ANCIENT EUROPE – GLOBAL GRIDS – EARTH & MOON – CRAFTS

HISTORY: ANCIENT EUROPE

Fabulous Fact

Archaeologists use names to designate certain "cultures" or people with certain similarities, but this does not mean that these people were related by blood, or custom, or even politically. It just means they had one or more defining characteristics that were similar, like language or pottery style.

Teaching Tip

Not every unit or subject you learn about has to involve lots of hands on projects. Essentials include books to read and a short writing assignment. Secondary are maps and timelines. Then if you have the energy and the desire, add in the activities to make it more memorable.

Famous Folks

Hanna Rydh was a Swedish archaeologist, instrumental in the excavation of several Swedish sites such as the Birka excavation and other pre-historic sites.

The people of northern Europe did not leave any written records, (at least none that we've found) so we only know a little bit about them. We know they lived in stone or wooden houses, depending on their environment. Lepenski Vir was a village near the Danube River where there were plenty of fish to catch and wooded land that could be used to build homes. In Skara Brae trees were scarce, so they built stone homes with stone furniture. Sweet Track was a marshy area, so the people there used wood not only to build their homes, but also for walkways that went from village to village so they could avoid walking through the wet marshes. We know they buried their important people, like chiefs, in underground barrows filled with riches. We know they made beautiful jewelry. We know they are the first who began to clear the vast forests that covered all of Europe, farm the land, and raise sheep and cattle. We know they mined for tin and collected amber, both of which they traded. But we don't know what stories or songs they told (though we can guess some of them), or the names of their great chiefs, or by what names they called their own tribes. We don't know much about their religions or why they built huge stone circles like Stonehenge.

Archaeological site at Skara Brae in the Orkney Islands. Photo by John Burka.

☺ ☺ **EXPLORATION: Ancient European Timeline**
The dates on this timeline are *very* approximate. No two sources agree on the exact details, and without written records these are all just educated guesses. Still, a timeline can help you see pro-

Ancient Europe – Global Grids – Earth & Moon – Crafts

gression and make general comparisons to other parts of the world. In general, southern Europe was more advanced than northern Europe during the same time periods. Printable timeline squares are at the end of this unit.

- 3300 BC Stone Avenue at Carnac constructed
- 3100-2500 BC Skara Brae is occupied
- 2800 BC Bronze Age begins
- 2500 BC Indo-Europeans begin to migrate from the Black Sea
- 2400 BC Work on Stonehenge begins
- 2400-1800 BC Bell-Beaker Culture
- 1700-600 BC Nordic Bronze Age cultures thrive (later become Germanic peoples)
- 1600 BC Stonehenge is complete
- 1000 BC Second wave of Indo-European migration
- 800 BC Iron Age begins

☺ ☻ ☻ **EXPLORATION: Ancient European Homes**
Make a model of an ancient European home. Use twigs from outside, Popsicle sticks, and glue. Most homes were small, with two rooms, one for the family and one for the animals. Get a rectangular baking dish; a disposable foil one would be ideal. Fill it with slightly moist dirt pressed firmly into the pan. Design a rectangular house, marking out the boundaries in the dirt. Place upright posts, either wood craft sticks or straight twigs, into the ground at intervals. You may want to secure it to a wooden frame under the dirt to make your posts more secure. Weave other twigs between the upright posts until you've built four walls, but remember to leave a space for the door, probably one on each end. You need one for the family and one for the animals.

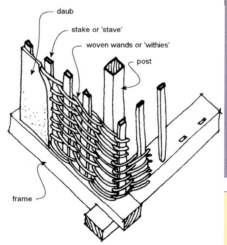

For the roof, glue or tie with string cross pieces to go between the side walls, then cover the roof with grass to represent the thatch. Roofs in most parts of Europe would probably have been pitched, with a peak, because Europe gets a lot of rain and snow. But design your roof the way you like. Now cover the outside of the house with mud. This style of house is called wattle and daub. Fences were also made by weaving sticks between upright posts.

Clearing It Up
Most people think of the Celts when they think of ancient Europeans. But the Celts were later than the Bronze Age people we're talking about in this unit. The Celts were a linguistic group of people known to the Romans and Greeks. We'll discuss them in detail in Unit 1-17.

Fabulous Fact
Namforsen is a site in northern Sweden where impressive rock carvings, both in terms of skill and number, can be found. There are pictures of animals, people, and boats.

Photograph by Hans Lindquist

Additional Layer
All over the world people still live with their animals inside their homes, or at least on one end of the house. Can you find out where in the world they do this?

Ancient Europe – Global Grids – Earth & Moon – Crafts

Additional Layer
Look for more great fairy tales from collections by Charles Perrault, the Brothers Grimm, and Andrew Lang. Paul Galdone's versions of many of the tales are charming and well-illustrated for young readers. Dover Publishers has inexpensive copies and libraries always have fairy tale collections. Look for the morals in the fairy tales and discuss the meanings.

Additional Layer
People have always made the most money through production and trade, including the Bronze Age Europeans. The wealthiest graves come with evidence of traded goods from far away. How does trade between nations benefit people?

Make yourself a wattle fence near your house to keep the animals from straying. You can make animals and people from clay or purchase plastic figures to go with your house.

😊 😊 😊 **EXPLORATION: A Bard's Tales**
Without a written language, information and stories had to be passed down orally. There were people whose job it was to travel from village to village and tell stories and sing songs to entertain and educate the people. They were called bards, and they were important guests in any household. They memorized long, epic poems and stories and told them word for word. It sounds tough, but with practice memories get better. Practice making your memory better by memorizing a poem or story. Many fairy tales like *Little Red Riding Hood*, and *Jack and the Beanstalk* are thought to be ancient enough to have been told around hearths in ancient European homes. Pick your favorite version of one of the tales and learn to tell it well enough to entertain an audience. Present it to friends or family.

EXPLANATION: Twice Upon A Time Tales
Whenever possible I try to dovetail our reading and writing together into one cohesive lesson. Of course, the obvious way to do this is simply to have kids write about what they're reading. *Twice Upon A Time Tales* are just a variation of this.

The basic concept is that kids read a story and then write their own version of it. And so I call them "Twice Upon A Time Tales." Start by brainstorming a list of simple story elements that could change.

- main character
- setting (this could be time/place/time period/all of those)
- several plot details
- ending
- role reversal of the bad guy/good guy
- conflict
- same character on a new adventure

Next, let kids take one or two changes and run with them. How would *Beauty and The Beast* be different with a male/female role reversal? (Handsome and the Beastess) *I know, I know. . . I may have made up the word "beastess."* What if the wolf had really been the good guy in *Little Red Riding Hood*? Could you tell the story of *Winnie the Pooh* using people instead of animals? How would YOU end the story of the *Little Match Girl*? Can you continue a Harry Potter tale? Perhaps tell of an adventure Harry's son has at Hogwarts? What if Johnny Appleseed had lived in a castle in medieval times? How would *Goldilocks and the Three Giraffes* go?

It doesn't matter so much what changes you make, but make a change and then let your pencil go like crazy. This isn't a new idea at all. We've been telling many of the same stories over the years, often just putting our own new spin on to them. Many classic story lines have been told time and time again. There are countless versions of classics, fairy tales, folk tales, and myths. Our stories have common threads, common themes, common protagonists, and common enemies.

Karen

☺ ☺ ☺ EXPLORATION: The Mystery of Stonehenge

The theories about how and why Stonehenge was built abound. We know that the stones were transported from 250 miles away on a land and water route. That means it must have been somehow significant and important to the builders. Getting them there was probably a bigger task than the actual building of the monument. One 12th century writer claimed it was built by Merlin the Wizard. Astronomers have tried to prove that it's a huge astronomical calendar. Some believe it's meant to be a grave marker for a cemetery. Still others believe it's a place of healing. What do you think it could have been used for? Write about your

---

Barbaric?

Many people believed the ancient Europeans to be backward and barbaric. I'm sure some of them were. Backward and barbaric people seem to be a staple of every society. But as a whole, archaeologists are slowly changing their minds about the Europeans. People who have functioning societies, great wealth, trade routes stretching across continents, and the skill to craft beautiful metal objects clearly are intelligent and capable.

Teaching Tip

Do some of the physical writing for young kids, who will be overwhelmed by the enormity of the task, when the purpose of the assignment is something other than learning to write.

On The Web

Go to the National Geographic website for an armchair expedition about Stonehenge. Search for "Stonehenge" and read the article called *If The Stones Could Speak*.
http://ngm.nationalgeographic.com/

Ancient Europe – Global Grids – Earth & Moon – Crafts

Additional Layer
Stonehenge has been the inspiration for another very unique sculpture. Built by Jim Reinders, Carhenge is a replica of the original built from classic American cars instead of huge monoliths. Go find out: how many cars it took to build it, how it is connected together, where it can be found, and what is written on it.

Druids?
Many people believe that the paganistic Druid religion was pervasive through Europe and practiced far, far back as the earliest European religion. The real evidence points to Druidism being confined to the extreme northwest of Europe and being more recent, as in the Celtic age. We don't know anything about the Bronze Age religions.

Additional Layers
A modern tale featuring old European burial mounds is *The Lord of the Rings* by J.R.R. Tolkien. Frodo and his friends are kidnapped and nearly killed by barrow weights as they pass through an old burial ground on their way to the Prancing Pony Inn.

theory in your writer's notebook. There's also a coloring sheet of Stonehenge in the printables section.

😊 🟢 **EXPLORATION: Burial Mounds**
Like the ancient Egyptians, death and burial were an important part of life to the ancient Europeans. They created large stone tombs with chambers and hallways to hold their dead. They buried the structures under mounds of earth. The tombs of the rich were filled with weapons, art, and treasures as well. Often burial grounds are found near stone circles like Stonehenge.

Create a model of a burial mound in the top of a shoe box, outside, or on a paper plate. Begin by placing stones inside to make a small cave. You may want to use clay to seal the stones together. Create some tiny swords or other treasures using tin foil to place within the caves. You may even want to put a small plastic toy figure inside to represent the body. Now cover the top with soil, creating a mound over the cave. Plant grass seed over the top and keep it moist for several weeks, allowing the grass to grow over and around the mound.

Ancient Europe – Global Grids – Earth & Moon – Crafts

☺ ☻ ● EXPLORATION: Dolmens and Avenues

Not all of the megalithic sites were stone circles like Stonehenge. Many sites of avenues, or rows of standing stones, exist all over Europe. There are also stone tombs called dolmens. Dolmens are exactly like the burial mounds in the previous exploration. One excellent site is called Carnac, after the modern village that stands there now. It is located in northwestern France, in the area known as Brittany. The Carnac site has avenues of standing stones, single stones, and dolmens. There are over three thousand stones in this one site, though many of them have been torn down and moved to make way for new developments.

Photographed by Steffen Heilfort.

There is a lot of controversy over the reason the ancients built these stone sites. The dolmens seem pretty straightforward as tombs, but why build avenues of thousands of stones? Were they ancient grave markers? Did they help the ancients foretell astrological occurrences? Were they a sort of calendar? Or were they ancient seismological instruments to warn of earthquakes? No one knows.

Search for "Carnac Stones" online to learn more and see photos, or ask your librarian if they have any books on standing stones or ancient Europe.

Imagine you are one of the ancients telling a foreigner about the stones. Describe them and explain what they are used for.

☺ ☻ ● EXPLORATION: Bell-Beaker Culture

Archaeologists name the ancient people they find evidence of after a distinctive feature of the culture or after a modern place name near the dig site. One of the ancient European cultures is called the Bell-Beaker Culture after the shape of the pottery these people made and used in their everyday lives. This style of pottery was found over most of western Europe. Most archaeologists believe that the people who made this pottery migrated and formed colonies all over Europe, bringing their pottery style with them. Others think the pottery style migrated, but not the people.

Vocabulary

Barrows are man-made hills or earth and stone containing burial places, usually of great chieftains or kings. They can also be called tumuli, kurgans, howes, mounds, huglegrab, or dolmens, depending where in the world they are.

Additional Layer

Stones play a roll in many old tales. Think about the story of young Arthur who had to pull a sword from a stone and anvil.

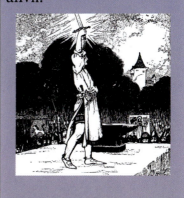

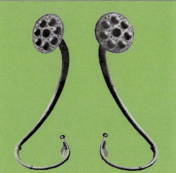

These are horns, called lurs, made of bronze and found in Denmark. These were probably used in war to signal to the troops.

Ancient Europe – Global Grids – Earth & Moon – Crafts

Fabulous Fact

Pottery often finds a special place in the hearts of archeologists. Its style is distinctive, its use is ubiquitous across cultures, and its remains last for hundreds and thousands of years.

Fabulous Fact

On the banks of the Humber River a man named Ted Wright discovered two boats buried in the soil. Another was found a little later by archaeologists. The boats turned out to date back to the Bronze Age. They are known as the Ferriby Boats.

Ferriby Boats Plaque, shared by Paul Glazzard

When searching for Bronze Age Europeans these terms may help:

Beaker Culture
Unetice Culture
Urnfield Culture
Tumulus Culture
Terramare Culture
Lusatian Culture
Yamna Culture
Catacomb Culture
Wessex Culture
Deverel-Rimbury Culture

The pottery looked like a big upside down bell. It was usually reddish or reddish brown in color and had horizontal bands, or lines ringing the beakers. The beakers appear to have been mostly used as drinking vessels, though there is evidence that they were used for other things like storing food, or as funeral urns. They had very thin sides and were smooth on the outside, resembling metal vessels made of gold or bronze.

Besides making beakers and drinking out of them, the Bell-Beaker people raised animals for a living. They would have had cattle and sheep. No doubt they did some farming and hunting as well.

And, like every other human culture on earth, they made war in their spare time. They were accomplished archers and had wrist guards. They used daggers. They were good at working metals including copper and gold. Many of the daggers found were made of copper, a soft metal, and were therefore probably ceremonial. The Bell-Beaker people also invented the halberd, a long stick with a dagger poking out of the end at right angles with the stick.

The Beaker people were the same ones who built the megalithic sites like Stonehenge, but nevertheless their religious and burial traditions seemed to differ from site to site. They were probably not one nation, but a series of cultures similar because of shared ancestry and trade ties, but we really don't know.

Color a map of the area their culture covered, then paste illustrations of their distinctive features all around the margin of the map as you explain them. Use the worksheet from the end of this unit and the completed version below.

ANCIENT EUROPE – GLOBAL GRIDS – EARTH & MOON – CRAFTS

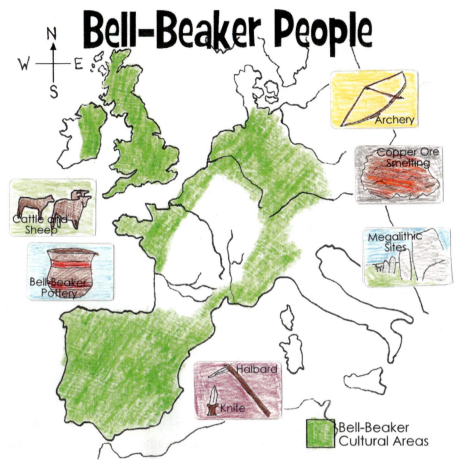

😊 😊 EXPLORATION: Indo-Europeans

Archaeologists like to talk about Indo-European languages and migrations and cultures, but what do they mean?

Scholars believe that languages belong to "families." A family is a group of languages that have enough similarities for scholars to assume that they had a common beginning. The Indo-European languages are thought to have begun before written history, roughly in the land between the Black Sea and the Caspian Sea. From there people spread out, making new colonies and conquering the people already in the land. Separated by distance and over the course of many, many years, their languages changed and morphed into completely new forms. The Indo-European languages eventually filled Europe, the Middle East and the Indian sub-continent. That is the basic theory. Exactly how much of it is true, we have no way of knowing. But there are some curious similarities between languages in far flung parts of the globe.

If this theory is correct, at least mostly, then most of Europe was populated by people who moved there from the steppes of the near east. They would have been the ancestors of the Bell-Beaker people, the ancestors of the Mycenaean people, Greeks, Romans,

Famous Folks

Marija Gimbutas was an American archaeologist, born in Lithuania. Most of her work took place in southeastern Europe and focused on the earliest of European cultures.

She brought forth the hypothesis that very ancient cultures were all matriarchal and woman centered, but were destroyed and subdued by the aggressive male dominated Kurgans.

The truth is that her evidence . . . well you really should read up on it and decide for yourself.

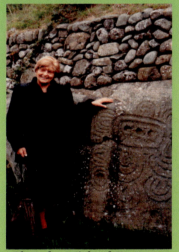

Photo by Michael Everson.

Fabulous Fact

Leaf bladed Bronze Age swords, made from bronze with 10% tin.

Photograph by Dbachmann

Ancient Europe – Global Grids – Earth & Moon – Crafts

Fabulous Fact
The Nebra sky disk was found near Nebra, Germany in 1999. The metals making up the disk are from Cornwall and Austria. No one knows what it was used for.

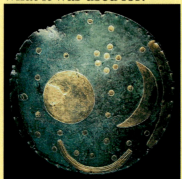

Photograph by Dbachmann

Additional Layer
This is a restored archeological site in Poland known as Biskupin. Learn more about it online.

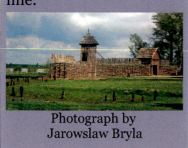

Photograph by Jarowslaw Bryla

Fabulous Fact
The largest known Bronze Age European city was at Vrable, Slovakia. The town was larger than the contemporary cities of Mycenae and Troy.

Britons, Celts, Vikings, Persians, Hittites, and so on. Draw a map showing this theory. Use the "Indo-European Migration Theory" map from the end of this unit.

Other peoples who would have been neighbors of these ancestors of Europe were the Semites to the south, who were the ancient Babylonians, and later the Hebrews and Arabs, among others. These Indo-European people used to be called Aryans because

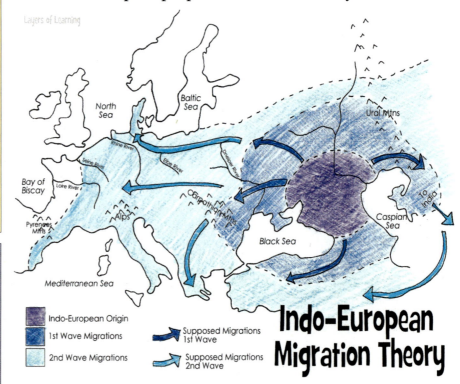

they were the ancestors of the people of the Persians, or Iranians. Their religion was originally polytheistic, but later one of their earliest spiritual leaders was Zoroaster, who taught them to worship the one true god and look forward to a savior. We will talk about him again in Unit 1-9.

☺ ☺ ☻ **EXPLORATION: Distaff and Spinning**
One of the oldest arts in the world is the spinning of yarn and the weaving of cloth. It's so old an art that we have no idea which people first invented it, but we do know that the ancient Europeans wore woven clothes made from wool and other fibers. It was the women who kept a people properly clothed and it was the women who used the distaff, a tool for spinning yarn from raw materials. The job was so important and so pervasive that even goddesses and queens engaged in it, as did the lowliest peasant.

A distaff was a paddle shaped board with a handle onto which the raw wool or cotton or flax was tied, then the spinner (person who

ANCIENT EUROPE – GLOBAL GRIDS – EARTH & MOON – CRAFTS

makes the yarn) would draw out long fibers and wind them onto a spindle.

If you have access to wool, you can actually spin some by hand and make your own yarn. You pull out bits of it at a time and twist it tightly as you go. You can also just buy yarn and take a closer look at it. Take a piece and unwind it, separate its pieces, and see how it looks like one fiber at first, but is actually made up of lots of spun threads.

If you'd like you can make some string figures using the yarn. They're lots of fun for all ages because of the challenge of getting it just right! For basic instructions on many different figures, visit www.alysion.org/string.htm or search for string figures online.

☺ ☺ ☺ EXPLORATION: Metal Working

Archaeologists have no idea how long ago people discovered metal ore and began to use it to make tools. The earliest and most common of metals was copper. But copper is soft and not very useful for chopping down a tree, plowing a field, or hacking away at enemies. It was around 2800 BC that Europeans first learned how to add tin to the copper to make a harder metal called bronze. Bronze could be used in armor, swords, plows, knives, and so on. We call the time when people used a lot of bronze *The Bronze Age*. The Bronze Age is different for every people on Earth because they all learned to mix copper and tin at different times.

You can demonstrate metal smelting with a simple activity. You will need sugar, molasses, and a mold. You can buy a candy mold or you can make a mold into any shape you like out of foil. Each of the kids could make their own foil mold to be shaped like an ancient European tool or ornament. The molds need to stay small though.

1. Put a cup of sugar into a saucepan. Tell the kids that it is a solid, but that if you heat it up enough it will become a liquid. Solid metal can also become a liquid if you heat it enough, but the temperatures are too high to be safe in a kitchen, so you will demonstrate with sugar.

Additional Layer

Look for great art depicting women with distaffs, such as:

Reine Berthe et les fileueses, 1888 by Albert Anker

The Spinner, 1873 by William-adolphe Bougeureau

The Spinner, 1892 by Wilhelm Maria Hubertus Leibl.

Compare the three paintings and notice the line, color, and mood of each. Learn about the history of the piece or more about the artist.

Ancient Europe – Global Grids – Earth & Moon – Crafts

Additional Layer

How is modern food preservation different from ancient? How is it the same?

Explanation

I feel like I've learned more since beginning to teach than I learned in my many years as a student. When my kids are focused on a subject I head to the library and fill our book bag with children's books on the subject, then I head over to the adult section and find one or two books about the same topics on my level. I try to challenge myself so I'm not just learning to prepare to teach, but I'm really learning (the librarian has given me many questioning stares about my book choices this year-- ancient history and astronomy are apparently NOT popular books for adults to check out in our small town.) My mind feels active and engaged when I'm memorizing poems, writing in my writer's notebook, painting a landscape, or reading a book about the ancients.

2. Turn the heat on the stove to medium and stir the sugar. Talk about the stuff ancient Europeans made with their metal. Ask the kids if they have any ideas.
3. The sugar will melt and turn nearly clear. Pour the liquid sugar into about half of the molds to harden. Explain that this is like the copper by itself. Allow to cool and harden.
4. Pour another cup of sugar into the pan, and this time add a tablespoon of molasses as well. The ancients found that a mixture with about ten percent tin added to the copper made the perfect bronze metal. Your sugar and molasses mixture represents this.
5. Heat and melt the sugar over medium temperature again, stirring constantly. While it heats discuss why a harder metal would be useful.
6. As soon as it is completely melted pour the liquid into the remaining molds. Allow it to harden.

Once the molds are hardened, take a picture of your tools and then you can eat them.

☺ ☺ ☺ **EXPLORATION: Making Food Last**

Keeping food from spoiling over a long period, like the winter, is a problem. Ancient people, including the early Europeans, used these methods to preserve food:

- <u>Drying.</u> They dried food in front of a fire, or just by laying it out in the sun. Getting rid of extra water keeps microbes from being able to grow and it's the microbes that spoil food. Some dried foods included berries, slices of fruits, thinly sliced meats and fish, and dried grains like wheat and barley.
- <u>Smoking.</u> If you hang meat in a small space filled with hot smoke it kills off any microbes present and cures and dries the meat so it doesn't grow new bacteria very easily.
- <u>Salting.</u> Salting or soaking meat in a brine solution or packing it in barrels with salt will keep it from spoiling. Microbes can't live in that amount of salt. But salt, in general, was expensive.
- <u>Cooling or freezing.</u> If you lived somewhere with cold winters you could butcher your meat in the late fall and keep it fresh by hanging it in an outbuilding in a cold place. It would freeze. At temperatures that low microbes can't grow. People also dug underground pits to store root vegetables like potatoes, turnips and carrots. Some people knew about evaporative cooling and would store butter or milk in clay jars they kept wet. As the water evaporates it cools the jar.
- <u>Fermentation.</u> Beer and wine were first made as a way to

ANCIENT EUROPE – GLOBAL GRIDS – EARTH & MOON – CRAFTS

preserve the harvest and ensure that a safe supply of water would be available. Everyone drank beer and wine, even children, but most of it was only mildly alcoholic, just enough to stave off harmful bacteria. Fermentation was also used in the making of cheese and yogurt.

- Pickling. To preserve vegetables long term they would sometimes be pickled, or placed in a vinegar and salt solution. They could be stored this way without ever having to be cooked or heated, thereby preserving the vitamin content.

As you teach kids about each of these methods of ancient food preservation have prepared samples of foods that have been preserved in each of these ways and let them try each food.

☺ ☺ ☺ EXPEDITION: Bridge Walk

Go find a bridge near you that you can walk along. While you're walking, talk about Sweet Track. Sweet Track was a wooden causeway, built over marsh lands. The farmers who built it wanted to be able to traverse the wetlands even when water would have prohibited them from crossing. Imagine how hard it would be to navigate around our nation if we had no bridges to help us cross water.

☺ ☺ EXPLORATION: Skara Brae

Go Visit the BBC website about Skara Brae. There's a terrific page for kids that lets them click on pictures to learn more about the evidence of ancient European peoples. It includes little videos and activities that kids can use to learn about this area and its people. Check it out at:
http://www.bbc.co.uk/scotland/learning/primary/skarabrae/

Explanation: Teaching With Arts and Crafts

Having a kid make a burial mound or ancient jewelry is fun, but you can really utilize that time by *teaching* as they work. After providing supplies and instructions, let the kids begin working while you begin teaching. Read them a book, tell them a story, or teach a concept during the project. Directly state what you hope they'll remember about the topic several times during the work period. Ask thought questions and keep the learning conversation going. Many kids actually learn far better while their hands are kept busy and moving, so don't waste the opportunity!

Karen

Additional Layer

Make a Venn diagram comparing the burial practices of the ancient Egyptians versus the ancient Europeans. How were they similar? Different? How did their values and beliefs play into their burial practices?

Ancient Europe – Global Grids – Earth & Moon – Crafts

Geography: Global Grids

Additional Layer
The Arctic and Antarctic circles don't stay put because the Earth's degree of tilt changes, or wobbles, over time. This wobbling happens mostly because the gravity of the moon makes the oceans slosh around (also known as tides) and that throws us a little off balance.

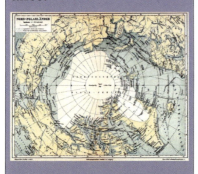

Writer's Workshop
When crossing the equator for the first time sailors, including some in the British Royal Navy and the U.S. Navy, go through an initiation ceremony. Some of the ceremonies were brutal, especially in the past. Sailors have been admitted to the sick bay or even died from them. The ceremonies held on tourist cruise ships are just for fun though. Design a fun equator crossing ceremony and describe it in your writer's notebook.

The purpose of a map is to tell us where things are. To help with that purpose geographers divide maps and globes into grids. With a grid you can give coordinates to precisely pinpoint where things are located. There are two main types of grid systems: latitude and longitude, and number and letter systems (also called alphanumeric grid references). These are labels written on the sides of flat paper maps.

Latitude and longitude are a coordinate system you can use to find any place on Earth. Globes and maps are marked with latitude and longitude lines, and GPS uses latitude and longitude to give exact directions. Directions like east and west rely on a starting point. For example, you might say, "Go east of the mountain and travel for 3 miles, then turn north and go another two miles." But latitude and longitude are exact directions. You can say the city is located at 2° E, 49°N and anyone can tell exactly which city you mean. (Use a world map and see if you can find the city.) Degrees are the largest unit of measure, but minutes and seconds are used as smaller increments within degrees. There are 180 degrees west, 180 degrees south, 90 degrees north, and 90 degrees south, just like in a circle. There are 60 minutes in each degree and 60 seconds in each minute, just like on a clock.

Atlases and some maps also use another system to help you find a particular place. They use letter and number coordinates. The letters usually run across the top and the numbers up the side. You can find everything in an atlas by looking at the index in the back, which lists everything the atlas contains in alphabetical order. In the index, you might find the river Sanaga under "S" and see that it is located at 124 G6. This means page 124, coordinate G6. You find the G across the bottom of the map and then move up the map until you get to the square 6. Where the G column and the 6 row converge is box G6. The river Sanaga is in this box. Look in the index of your atlas to find which country the river Sanaga is in.

Ancient Europe – Global Grids – Earth & Moon – Crafts

☺ ☺ ☺ EXPLORATION: A Global Grid

Hold up a ball or other round object and point to a random spot on it. Ask someone to describe the marked spot without touching it or saying "right there." After some attempts, explain that without reference points it's difficult to describe the location of a place. Early mapmakers made a grid system on the earth so they could easily and accurately describe locations.

Now wrap a piece of yarn around the center of the sphere to mark the equator. The equator is an imaginary line. If you were really there, you wouldn't see any visible evidence of it. It's a line we've created to describe that location on the earth. It helps us divide the earth into hemispheres so we can accurately describe our earth. You may also want to point out the Tropic of Cancer and the Tropic of Capricorn, parallels of latitude (called parallels because they are parallel to the equator), the Prime Meridian, the International Date Line, and longitude lines. All of these are part of the giant grid system of imaginary lines we've created on the globe to describe real locations on earth.

Next, using round balloons and permanent markers, each person can draw and label the important lines on the balloon. You may want to include the basic outlines of the continents in green. Use orange for the equator, yellow for the tropics, and pink for a few other parallels. Use purple for the prime meridian, brown for the international date line, and black for the longitude lines.

☺ ☺ EXPLORATION: A Classroom Grid

This activity can be done inside or outside. Use chalk lines or masking tape to create a large grid on the floor. Label the coordinates with either degrees latitude and longitude or the map grid system (A1, B10, etc.). Place a different object inside each of the grid squares. Choose an object within the grid and write its coordinates. Give the coordinates to someone else and see if they can determine what your secret object is. Go back and forth finding secret objects. Point out that we can only write coordinates for objects that aren't moving. We can describe where Iceland is, but we can't describe where a flying airplane is using coordinates, at least not for long!

☺ EXPLORATION: Latitude and Longitude

Use this word association trick to help your kids remember which is latitude and which is longitude: Latitude you can climb like a ladder. Longitude are long from the very top to the very bottom. Teach them how to find a place on a globe using coordinates. Use a globe to find which lakes are at each of these coordinates: 15° E 14°N; 60°E 45°N; 105°E 54°N; 98°W 52°N, 0°S 32°E

Fabulous Fact

The Prime Meridian is located at Greenwich, England because the Royal Observatory is there. It was the British who standardized the global grid system during their age of colonization.

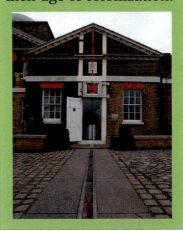

Fabulous Fact

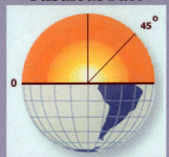

Lines of latitude are drawn from a center point inside the earth to the surface.

Besides the lines of latitude being affected by the roundness of the globe, they are also affected by the globe not being perfectly spheroid. It's a bit fatter at the equator and flattened at the poles; this affects the placement of the lines of latitude on the surface.

Ancient Europe – Global Grids – Earth & Moon – Crafts

Fabulous Fact
Most of the lines that people make on earth are imaginary only, there is no physical evidence of them on the surface of the earth, but the latitude line that divides Canada from the United States at the 49th parallel is actually visible because the border patrol cut down and maintain a long swath of forest from the Pacific to the Great Lakes.

Additional Layer
The game *Battleship* uses a grid system of coordinates. Play it.

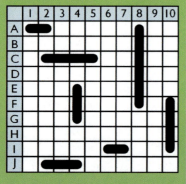

EXPLANATION: Latitude and Longitude Memory Aids
Some kids have a tough time remembering which direction latitude goes and which direction longitude goes. Here are some tips to help them remember.

1. Use a wood craft stick. On one side write LONGITUDE vertically and on the other side write LATITUDE horizontally. This can be used as a tool when doing map work until they remember it on their own.

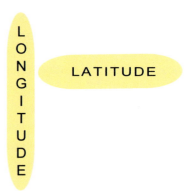

2. This little chant works wonders: Longitude lines go up and down, latitude lines go round and round.

3. For visual learners, draw a simple sketch of a globe with a spider sitting on top. His legs fall down and make the longitude lines. Now draw another simple globe with a ladder spanning it. The rungs of the ladder form the latitude lines.

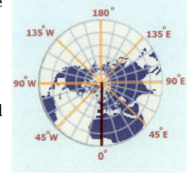

4. You can also remember which is which by the way your mouth moves when you say the words "latitude" and "longitude." When you say "laaaaaaaaatitude" your mouth goes wide and side to side. When you say "looooooooooooongitude" your mouth gets big up and down.

☺ EXPLORATION: City Hunt
Use an atlas index to find these cities: Perugia, Hamadan, Andong, Rosario, Honiara, Suva, Dunedin, Khartoum, Windhoek, Nukus, Poznan, Burgos, and Quemado.

☺ ☺ ☺ EXPLORATION: Ribbons on the Grid
Use the world map printable for this exploration. You'll need several colors of ribbon, some glue, and scissors. Glue a purple ribbon to the equator. Explain that if we were standing on the equator, we wouldn't see a line at all. We have just put an imaginary line on our maps to represent the line that divides the globe in half, the same distance from the north pole to the south. Now glue a yellow ribbon on the prime meridian and explain what it is. Finally, add some other *lines of latitude and longitude as you discuss why we have these on our maps. Try these:

Ancient Europe – Global Grids – Earth & Moon – Crafts

Orange line (20 degrees North, 80 degrees East)
Green line (40 degrees South, 140 degrees West)
Brown line (80 degrees North, 160 degrees East)
Red line (80 degrees South, 40 degrees East)
Blue line (60 degrees North, 80 degrees West)

*Latitude lines are always listed before longitude lines in coordinates.

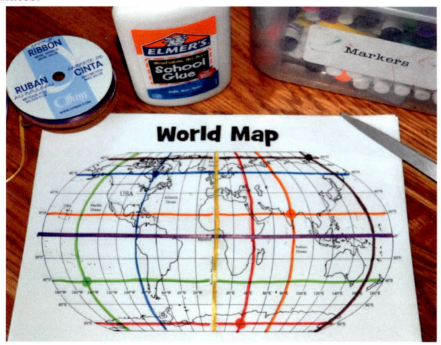

Finally, use markers to locate some important places to your family like your home town or places you've visited. Identify their coordinates.

😊 😊 EXPEDITION: Geo-caching

If you own or can borrow a hand held GPS device try geo-caching, a challenge to find a particular place on earth where a "prize" is hidden. It's like a high tech treasure hunt. There are caches (or prize spots) all over the planet. Go to www.geocaching.com for more information and to get coordinates near you.

😊 😊 EXPLORATION: Hemispheres

Using a globe, map, or atlas, list locations on the globe. You can use familiar countries, continents, landmarks, and famous cities. You can also give coordinates. Once the student has found the location, they have to say whether it's in the northern or southern hemisphere. Make it a game and see how fast they can determine which hemisphere the location is in. Once they've got north and south, work on east and west.

Additional Layer

Geometry on a 3-dimensional object is very different than geometry on a flat plane, like your piece of paper. For example, the formula for the area of a triangle on a flat plane is ½ base x height. But on a sphere the formula doesn't work. Since the area is curved, it will be greater than the area of a similar triangle drawn on a flat plane. On a regular triangle the sum of the angles is always 180°, but on a spheroid triangle the sum is greater than 180°. On the triangle in the photo the angles add up to 203°. Try it yourself. Draw three points on a round playground ball. (Use a wet erase marker if you want the ink to come off later.) Connect the dots using a flexible tape measure to make your lines straight. Then use a protractor to check the angle measures.

Ancient Europe – Global Grids – Earth & Moon – Crafts

Additional Layer
While the Arctic is ocean surrounded by land masses, the Antarctic is a land mass surrounded by oceans. This makes the two regions very different. Research to find out how they are different and more about why.

Additional Layer
Though no one lives south of the Antarctic Circle on a permanent basis, there are several towns north of the Arctic Circle. Find out where they are and learn what it is like to live in that extreme environment.

Ice ridges in the Beaufort Sea off the northern coast of Alaska.

Fabulous Fact
Degrees aren't always accurate enough. Minutes and seconds are smaller units of latitude and longitude that can help us find a location.

Look up the *exact* location of your town.

☺ ☻ EXPLORATION: Equator Heat and Cold Poles

Read *The Polar Express* by Chris Van Allsburg. Point out what the whether is like at the North Pole. Now read parts of Mark Twain's *Following the Equator: A Journey Around the World* as he describes some of the hottest places on earth. Why is it hot near the equator and cold near the poles? Use your globe and a yellow balloon that represents the sun to show that the equator is actually nearer the sun and gets more direct light and heat. This creates the temperature variation.

Using the world map at the end of this unit, have students draw a climate map showing the hotter temperatures in red at the equator. Progressively show cooler and cooler temperatures as you work towards the poles.

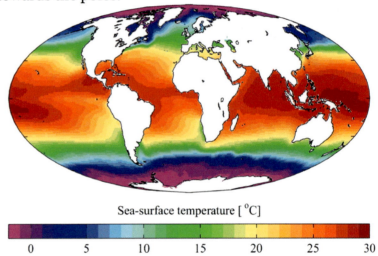

☺ ☻ EXPLORATION: What Should I Wear?

Give each student a world map with latitude lines on it. Give clues and have them tell you what you'll need to pack in your suitcase. A coat? Shorts? Keep in mind that while it's summer in the northern hemisphere, it's winter in the southern hemisphere and vice versa. If you're near enough to the equator or to the poles, it doesn't matter what month it is! What type of clothing would be appropriate for these locations and seasons:

- 60°N latitude in January
- 10°N latitude in February
- 40°N latitude in August
- 40°S latitude in July
- 70°S latitude in September
- 70°N latitude in May
- 15°S latitude in October

Ancient Europe – Global Grids – Earth & Moon – Crafts

☺ ☺ ☺ **EXPLORATION: Living on the Equator**
Trace your finger along the equator and name some countries that touch the equator. Use a map or a globe to find them and make a list. Now create an Equator Encyclopedia. Choose several countries that will each get one section of information about it. Topics may include: the country's geography, location (latitude and longitude), population, climate, health, politics, education, economy, and a brief history. Once all the information is compiled about each country, combine them and bind your Equator Encyclopedia. You may want to have each kid do one or two countries, but combine the work of everyone into one book.

☺ ☺ **EXPLORATION: Drawing Lines of Latitude**
Begin with a circle drawn on a sheet of paper. Use a compass to make the circle. Bisect the circle in half. The line you drew is the equator, label it with "equator" and "0°." Now place the origin of a protractor in the exact center of your circle on the equator. This point is like a spot in the exact center of the earth. From this point we mark angles up from the equator using the protractor. Make a mark along the circumference of the circle at each of these angles: 15, 30, 45, 60, 75, 90. Mark these angles up and down from the equator on all four quarters of the circle. Now use a ruler to connect the marks made on the circumference of the circle to the marks made on the opposite side. These are your lines of latitude.

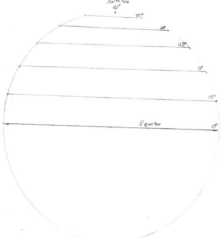

Compare your lines to the lines on a globe. On the globe the lines are equidistant from one another, but the lines on your flat piece of paper get closer together at the poles. If you drew your lines on a round ball would they come out equidistant?

Additional Layer
Learn more about tides which are caused by the Moon's pull on Earth.

Famous Folks
Nevil Maskelyne, Astronomer Royal, was important in the determination of latitude and longitude lines worldwide, particularly in relation to the ability of ships at sea to determine their location.

Additional Layer
Lacking a reliable way to determine longitude while at sea, thousands of sailors suffered and died in shipwrecks and from scurvy while lost at sea. This prompted the British Crown to offer a prize to the one who solved the problem of determining longitude. The story of this contest and the man who (almost) won it is told in *The Longitude Prize* by Joan Dash and in the movie "Longitude" from A&E.

ANCIENT EUROPE – GLOBAL GRIDS – EARTH & MOON – CRAFTS

On The Web

Go to www.KidsGeo.com and search for "latitude longitude game" for more fun practice with this concept.

For a fun printable "board" game from Scholastic go to http://teacher.scholastic.com/lessonrepro/reproducibles/profbooks/MessageinBottle.pdf

Visit www.NationalGeographic.com/expeditions and search for "crack the code," another fun game to learn latitude and longitude skills.

Memorization Station

Memorize the major lines of latitude and longitude and their degree designations.

Fabulous Fact

Eartha, in Maine, is the largest globe in the world at 41.5 feet in diameter.

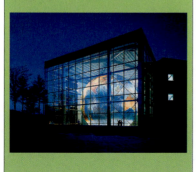

☺ ☻ EXPLORATION: Drawing Lines of Longitude.

Draw a circle with a compass. The center point is one of the poles, either north or south. All around the circumference of the circle draw the degrees of latitude in 10 degree increments. Up to 180 from a zero line, which you can randomly choose. Draw lines from your points along the circumference to the center point. These are your lines of longitude. Each line gets closer at the center (or pole) and further at the circumference (or equator). You can try this on a sphere, like a playground ball, by using a flexible tape measure to draw the lines. Just mark a point at the pole then use a protractor to make other marks for the degrees.

☺ ☻ EXPLORATION: Free-hand World Map

Start with a blank piece of paper. Fold it in half the long way. Open it back up and trace over the fold line. This is the equator. Next, draw a parallel line near the top and bottom of the paper. These are the arctic and antarctic circles. Now draw lines 1/3 of the way between the equator and arctic circles. These are the Tropic of Cancer and the Tropic of Capricorn. Fold your paper in half the other way. Unfold it and trace along this line; this is the Prime Meridian. Now, while looking at a map of the world, draw the continents on. It's easiest if you use a map which puts the Prime Meridian in the center of the page.

Practice doing this map from time to time until your kids know these important lines and basic shapes of the continents by heart.

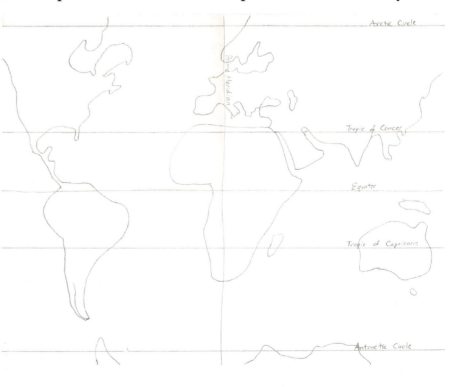

25

SCIENCE: EARTH & MOON

Earth is perfectly placed for life. It's not too hot, not too cold. It's tipped just right to create a healthy seasonal cycle for plants and animals. It has an atmosphere that is both simple and complex at the same time – a super thin sheet of gases in just the right mix that both create a medium for life and protect that life from the dangers of outer space (dangers like solar radiation and bombardment by meteors). The atmosphere also keeps the heat of the earth perfect, trapping just enough (we call this the greenhouse effect), and also creates a way for water to become fresh and clean again to be used over and over. Speaking of water, it is present on earth in just the right amounts and is one of the few substances that is less dense as a solid. Imagine if ice sank to the bottom. Many of the lakes and oceans of the world would be perpetually frozen. The inside of the earth, a hot, constantly changing mix of minerals, makes the earth itself living and changing instead of cold and barren. As interesting as the other planets are, Earth is by far the most beautiful and varied.

Our moon adds to the perfection of Earth. Its pull keeps the oceans moving and churning instead of dead and stagnant. It gives us cycles of periods (roughly months) to help us tell time, even changing its shape as it goes like an automatic clock. In the last century, the race for humans to get to the Moon fulfilled the fantasies of millenia and fascinated the whole world for a decade. The moon's light, particularly when near full, gives light to even our nights. One of the most fascinating events of ancient and modern times is a solar eclipse, when the moon passes directly between the earth and the sun, blocking the sun's light. If you get a chance to witness one, you won't want to miss it.

😊 😊 EXPLORATION: The Guts of the Earth

Earth has a solid core surrounded by molten lava and then covered over with a thin crust. Draw a picture of the inside structure of the earth. Or better yet, use clay or play dough to model the structure of the earth.

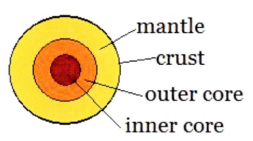

😊 😊 😊 EXPERIMENT: Belly Bulge

The earth is almost a sphere, but not quite. It bulges at the equator. To see why, try this: Make a paper sphere with two long strips of paper (or four shorter strips taped together to make two

---

Famous Folks

The first person to make an accurate map of the moon was Wilhelm Beer, an amateur astronomer from Germany (1777-1850)

Additional Layer

This is one of those areas where faith and scientific speculation seem to conflict. Take the opportunity to teach your child what you believe about the formation of the earth and whether you believe in random chance or creation.

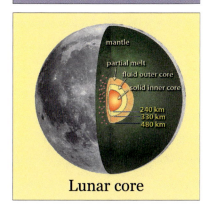

Lunar core

Ancient Europe – Global Grids – Earth & Moon – Crafts

Memorization Station

The Moon
by Robert Louis Stevenson

The moon has a face like the clock in the hall;

She shines on thieves on the garden wall,

On streets and fields and harbor quays,

And birdies asleep in the forks of the trees.

The squalling cat and the squeaking mouse,

The howling dog by the door of the house,

The bat that lies in bed at noon,

All love to be out by the light of the moon.

But all of the things that belong to the day

Cuddle to sleep to be out of her way;

And flowers and children close their eyes

Til up in the morning the sun shall arise.

long strips) at right angles to each other. Tape them together, then stick a pencil up through the center of one of the axes. Spin the pencil between your hands. Watch the shape of the spinning papers. The center bulges out further than the rest of the sphere. The earth is the same way, the center bulges because of the spin.

 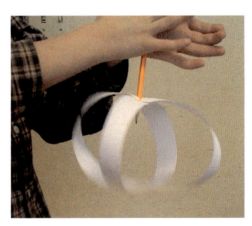

☺ ☺ ☺ EXPERIMENT: Precession

Because of the bulging equator, the earth doesn't spin in perfect, even circles. It wobbles. The wobbling is called precession. Precession for the earth takes a long time, about 26,000 years for the axis to make one complete circle.

You can show how precession works with a top. You can use one you have around or you can build one with Lego axles, wheels, and gears. Spin it and watch how the weight spins and wobbles slightly on the axis. (This is a good time to explain what an axis is too.)

☺ ☺ EXPLORATION: Days and Seasons

Use a flashlight, a ball or globe, and a smaller ball to show the seasons, days, and eclipses. The sun is represented by the flashlight, the earth is the largest ball, and the moon is the smaller ball.

<u>Seasons:</u> The earth tilts in relation to the sun, meaning that in the summer the north pole is tilted toward the sun, and in the winter the south pole is tilted toward the sun.

Ancient Europe – Global Grids – Earth & Moon – Crafts

<u>Day and night</u>: During the day your location on Earth faces the sun; at night your location on Earth is turned away from the sun. When it is day at your house, what is happening in Russia?

<u>Eclipses</u>: An eclipse happens when the earth, moon and sun all line up in a straight line. Sometimes the moon is between the earth and the sun; this is a solar eclipse. Sometimes the earth is between the sun and moon. This is a lunar eclipse. The eclipse is happening because the view of one celestial body is blocking the view of the other.

Galileo's drawings of moon phases, 1616.

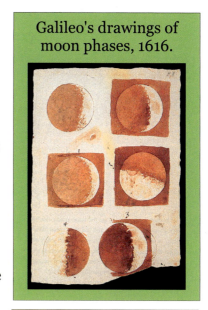

☻ ☻ ☻ **EXPERIMENT: Solstice Map**
The solstice is the time when the sun appears to stop and reverse its course either north or south. The summer (or northern) solstice occurs on June 20th or 21st. The winter (or southern) solstice occurs on December 21st or 22nd. The solstice occurs because the earth is tilted. The moment the sun is facing the north pole most directly is the summer solstice. The north pole has 24 hours of sunlight during this time. The opposite is true of the winter solstice.

On The Web
NASA's Eclipse Website has information about all the solar and lunar eclipses – past, present, and future.
www.eclipse.gsfc.nasa.gov/eclipse.html

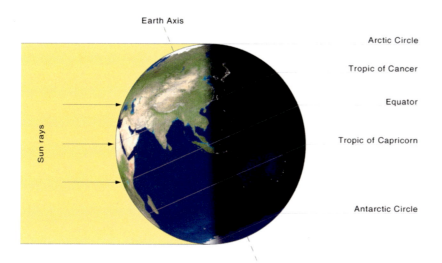

Image compiled by Przemyslaw Idzkiewicz

Once a month for the next six months note where on the horizon the sun sets each time. Map it in relation to your house. Draw a footprint of your house (just a rectangle showing location is fine) and mark how many degrees north or south of your house the sun is setting. Write the date next to each entry.

☻ ☻ ☻ **EXPLORATION: Equinox Eggs**
The equinox is the time when the sun is exactly overhead at the equator. As the earth tilts first toward, and then away from the sun, the sun crosses the equator twice a year, once in the spring

Fabulous Fact
Popular winter solstice celebrations include Christmas, Yalda, Saturnalia, Hanukkah and Yule.

Popular summer solstice celebrations include the feast of St. John and Midsummer Festival.

Ancient Europe – Global Grids – Earth & Moon – Crafts

Additional Layer
Because of precession, the north star has changed over time. Now it is the star we call Polaris. When the pyramids were built it was a star called Alpha Draconis.

The Great Pyramid at Giza was made to face exactly toward the north star and it did. Too bad the north star "moved."

Duat is the art of placing objects on earth to mirror objects in the sky. It was practiced in ancient Egypt. The pyramids line up with the constellation Orion, face due north, and cast no shadow on the spring equinox. At midnight on the autumn equinox the Great Pyramid points up directly at the star Alycone, thought by some to be the center of the universe as our sun is the center of the solar system.

Additional Layer
In Roman mythology the god was called Jupiter. The same god was known by a different name in Greek mythology – Zeus.

Most of our planets and many moons are named from Roman mythology.

and once again in the autumn. The spring equinox is on June 20th or 21st and the autumn equinox occurs on September 21st or 22nd.

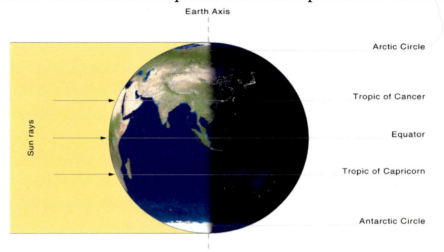

Image compiled by Przemyslaw Idzkiewicz and shared on Wikimedia Commons.

A long held myth relating to the equinox is that on either the autumn or spring equinox a raw egg can be balanced on end, but not on any other day. Give it a try. Create a graph of data and attempt to balance an egg on end before, during and after the equinox to see what will happen. (The point of this experiment is to generate interest in the equinox and to introduce the concept, so ham it up.)

☺ ☺ ☺ **EXPLORATION: "Moon" or "moon"?**
There are many, many moons just within our solar system. Many have been given names. Jupiter has at least 63 moons, many of which are named for daughters, lovers, and other "relatives" of the Roman god, Jupiter. Ganymede, Callisto, Io, and Europa are the 4 largest of Jupiter's moons. Our moon doesn't have a fancy name like that; we call it the Moon (we can use a capital M if we are using it as its name). Similarly, other stars are called "suns" but our star is the Sun (with a capital S). Earth, moon, and sun are all seen with small letters most often, but when used as a name you can choose to capitalize them if you want to.

Galileo was the first person to see the moons of Jupiter and call them "moons." They were similar to our moon in the way they orbited around their planet, so he used this familiar term to describe what he had found. Now we refer to all moons in that way. Do you think it makes the moon seem more or less important because it's called "the moon" instead of having a different name like the other moons?

Ancient Europe – Global Grids – Earth & Moon – Crafts

Take a piece of paper and fold it in half. Draw Earth with the Moon going around it on one side. Now draw another planet and its moons (or at least some of them) on the other side. Add labels to your drawings to describe what you have pictured. Now write at least 5 things about the Moon on the first side and 5 things about the moons on the other side. What do they have in common? How are they different?

😊 🟢 ⚫ **EXPEDITION: Moon Gazing**
On a night with a full moon, go out with binoculars or a telescope and a moon map and identify some of the features on the surface of the moon. Older kids can draw their own moon map, identifying features as they go.

😊 🟢 ⚫ **EXPLORATION: Lunar Myths**
Read some myths about the moon. Many peoples have seen pictures on the face of the moon. Some Native American tribes saw a rabbit and most modern Americans see a face, which we call *the man in the moon*.

Full Moon, Photographed by Luc Viator, 2006

Famous Folks
Harrison Schmidt was a NASA astronaut and geologist who walked on the moon.

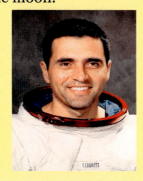

Fabulous Fact
Saturn's equinox occurs every 14 years. The next one will be April 30, 2024.

Additional Layer

Many cultures have deified the sun and moon. In Norse mythology they are named Mani and Sol. The female, Sol, representing the sun.

Ancient Europe – Global Grids – Earth & Moon – Crafts

Additional Layer
In 1967, the *Outer Space Treaty* was entered into by the U.S. and Russia, the two countries involved in the Space Race. The treaty says that the moon is the province of all mankind and can only be used for peaceful purposes.

Additional Layer
Use the printable template at the end of this unit to make a mobile.

😊 😊 😊 **EXPLORATION: Lunar Base**
Make a lunar base. Use a piece of poster board or plywood as your moon surface. Color or paint the surface gray. Decide what you'll need to survive for a year on the moon. Using egg carton pieces, empty food packaging, Styrofoam cups, other saved stuff, and cardboard, build modules for the different needs you'll have. What will you do for food, water, air, and living space? Paint it all out in the colors you like.

CJ's Moon base

😊 😊 **EXPERIMENT: Planets and Temperature**
How does distance from the sun affect a planet's temperature?

You need:
2 thermometers
A light (like a desk lamp)

1. Set up the lamp on a table and then set one thermometer close to the lamp on the table (just a few inches from the base) and the other thermometer a little further away (a few feet from the base).
2. Turn the lamp on and record the temperatures on each thermometer every minute for about 15 minutes. Which one is hotter? Which stays cooler?

The closer thermometer is like a planet that is closer to the sun. It gets more heat because it absorbs more energy at the closer distance. Less of the light's rays (and therefore less energy) get to

Ancient Europe – Global Grids – Earth & Moon – Crafts

the thermometer that is a few feet away, so it stays cooler. What would happen to us and the earth if it were closer or further from the sun?

😊 😊 EXPERIMENT: Moonlight

This experiment needs to be done in a dark room or at night. You'll need:
- a small mirror
- a flashlight

Question: Does the moon give light?
Procedure: In the dark, shine the flashlight at the mirror. See how it appears to light up? Now turn off the flashlight. The mirror is no longer lit. The mirror doesn't give its own light, but it can reflect the light of the flashlight. This is just like the moon. It looks like it's glowing at night because the light from the sun is reflecting off of it. If the sun weren't shining on it, it would not be able to glow on its own. The moon doesn't give off its own light. We only have moonlight because we have sunlight.

😊 😊 EXPEDITION: Apollo 13

This is a really fun armchair expedition. Watch the 1995 *Apollo 13* movie and go along with the astronauts who attempted to land on the moon from the NASA Apollo 13 Mission. Though there are minor differences between the show and real life, the events are portrayed fairly accurately. For the full picture, listen to the commentary by Jim and Marilyn Lovell on the special features portion of the show. It's rated PG and has mild profanity.

😊 😊 😊 EXPEDITION: Kennedy Space Center

A visit to the Kennedy Space Center at Cape Canaveral, Florida is an unforgettable one.

There are all kinds of exhibits, an IMAX theater, giant rockets, simulators, and a fascinating tour. You'll get to talk to real astronauts, see what the first mission control room was like, see what it feels like to walk on the moon, and walk through a rocket garden with real rockets.

Elizabeth at the Kennedy Space Center, Cape Canaveral, Florida

Writer's Notebook

Neil Armstrong was the very first man to walk on the moon. The mission, though well-planned, was uncertain. No one had ever done anything like the Apollo 11 crew was attempting, and no one knew just what to expect, or whether or not the astronauts would return home alive and safe. Read about their voyage to learn what it was like. *Spacebusters: The Race To The Moon* by Philip Wilkinson is a good book to start with.

It must have been a pretty amazing moment as Armstrong climbed down the ladder from the Eagle landing craft and set foot on the moon, the first person ever to do so. He said, "One small step for a man, one giant leap for mankind." What do you think he meant by that? If YOU were the first person to walk on the Moon (or Mars or another planet!), what would YOU say for all the world to hear? Write about it in your writer's notebook.

Additional Layer

Learn more about astronauts and the first Moon landing. You can see a video of the first Moon landing on You Tube.

THE ARTS: CRAFTS

Here's A Useful Art

Door carving from Château de Fontainebleau, France

Useful art is just art that is meant to be used. Useful art was a trademark of the ancients. From ancient times people have been making things they needed, like weapons or dishes, and then also decorating them to create not only useful, but beautiful items too. We have many modern items of useful art today too. Take a look in your kitchen cupboards. Most likely you'll see lots of colors, patterns, and designs on your dishes.

Byzantine Bowl dating from the 11th century, photograph by Giovanni Dall'Orto

Additional Layer

Architecture just may be one of the most common useful arts. If we didn't care how a building looked or functioned, we wouldn't go to all the trouble of crafting such varied designs.

Architects take great care to consider not just engineering, but also beauty and function.

Marble Cathedral in Sienna, Italy

Browse through the projects below, check out a few crafting books from the library and choose one or two projects to focus on for the next two or three weeks. Don't try to do too much at once. Before a craft can really be enjoyed some proficiency must be gained in it. So instead of making five projects in different areas, you may want to choose one area and make several projects.

Modern Egg Chair. Photograph by Scott Anderson

Ancient Europe – Global Grids – Earth & Moon – Crafts

☺ ☺ ☺ **EXPLORATION: Art Hunters**
Use this activity to introduce the idea of useful art, then pick a project together. Look around your home. Make a list of 10-20 things you find that are useful art – things that are both beautiful or decorative and also can be used for a purpose. (Think furniture, home decor, clothing, jewelry, dishes, or parts of the actual architecture of your home.) Keep an open mind. On my home, my house numbers are useful art. They are lovely and they also help people find my home using my address. Sure, I could have used black spray paint to label my home, but instead I built this frame, inlaid the tile, and then adhered decorative vinyl numbers – useful and definitely more attractive than the spray paint option.

Additional Layer
Learning to write letters in fancy or special styles can be art too. Learn about calligraphy, graphic design, or other lettering styles.

Additional Layer
Art and other disciplines often intersect when you work on useful art. Think about how cooking and art intersect. How do computer science and art intersect? What about gardening and art? Science and art?

French formal garden in the Loire Valley

☺ ☺ ☺ **EXPLANATION: Two Ways of Sculpting**
There are 2 basic ways to sculpt. Before actually sculpting, each of these can be practiced with a small ball of clay.

1. The pinch and pull method: Begin with a sphere of clay. Pull out ears and a nose. Pinch inward to form eyes and mouth. Don't break off any of the clay; instead, just manipulate the ball in one piece.
2. The Additive Method: Start with a smaller sphere of clay (reserve some on the side.) Use the reserved clay to form a little nose, ears, and lips. Before sticking them on to the sphere, use a fork to rough up the surface a little so the clay sticks better. A bit of water on your fingertips will help smooth out the wrinkles and bumps as you go.

☺ ☺ ☺ **EXPLORATION: Sculpt a Pinch Pot**
Using clay, sculpt a simple bowl, pot, or vase. You pinch the sides with your fingers as you sculpt, trying to keep all the sides even in

Additional Layer
Advertisers and merchandisers are particularly interested in the effects that colors and packaging have on consumers. How would you market a healthy product versus a product aimed at attracting children?

Ancient Europe – Global Grids – Earth & Moon – Crafts

Explanation

When working with any kind of 3-D art (like sculpture), it can be fun to have kids try to work by *feel*.

Here's an example of what I may do during this unit:

First, put a blindfold on each child. Set out several teacups, tea pots, saucers, and bowls. Let the children touch them and each choose one they like best. Ask them to describe what their object feels like in the most vivid language they can. They are describing the shape, texture, thickness, and material. Next, give each kid (blindfolds still on!) a ball of clay. Challenge them to replicate what they felt.

Working by touch instead of relying just on sight will challenge kids to have to think and create in new ways.

Karen

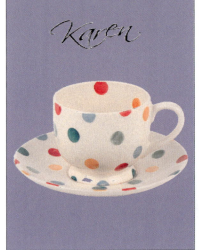

thickness. If you'd like you can use a toothpick or other gadgets to draw designs on the outside of your vessel. Make a pattern or repeat the textures to unify the pot. Let it dry in the sun (or use the heat from a fire) like the ancients did. After it's dry, apply paint or glaze for more decoration. If you use just one color of paint it will really bring out the textures and patterns you drew.

What could you use it for? Does your texture create unity within your piece? Did you use the element of line in your design? Are the sides of your pot nice and even in thickness? Does it actually hold liquids?

CJ with the pinch pot he made.

😊 😊 😊 EXPLORATION: Make it Pretty

Look around your home and find something useful that isn't particularly attractive. It may be a picture frame, a hand held mirror, a pair of shoes, a shirt, a small piece of furniture, or just a simple notebook. Now modify it so it suits your taste and personality. You might paint it; decoupage something on to its surface; or add stickers, ribbon, or buttons. You may glue tiles on to it, sand and stain it, or dye it another color.

😊 😊 EXPLORATION: Simple Weaving

Weaving is one popular form of useful art. Baskets, rugs, and clothing can all be woven from basic string or yarn. You can make a woven belt with just a few items:

- 4-5 plastic drinking straws
- a 5" x 7" piece of tough cardboard
- tape
- yarn

First, measure 5 pieces of yarn long enough to go around the belt wearer's waist (leave some extra at the end for tying knots). Tie the strands together at one end and then tape it to the cardboard just below the knot. Slide each straw up as far as you can along

Ancient Europe – Global Grids – Earth & Moon – Crafts

the pieces of string. The yarn in the straw is called the warp. Now tie a separate piece of yarn on to the tied end. This is your weft. Weave the yarn over and under the straws, going back and forth over the straws. The straws are there so your pieces don't get tangled up and twisty. As the weaving progresses, slide the straws down along the strands so they stay just under where you're weaving. You can change colors by cutting the weft yarn and tying on a new piece as often as you'd like.

Now you've created a beautiful, and useful artistic belt. Wear it well.

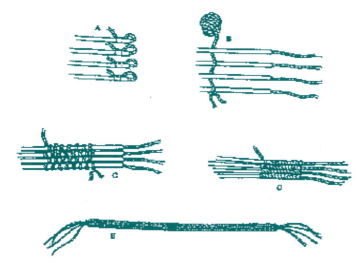

☺ ☺ ☺ **EXPLORATION: Wet Chalk**

One of the main things people use to make useful things beautiful is to simply add color. Look in any home decorating magazine or book and you're sure to see lots of colors of all tones and hues. We don't need that color to hold up the walls; we use it to make our homes beautiful.

Different colors actually have an effect on the way you feel. Researchers have generally found the following to be accurate:

- pink – soothing, affectionate, romantic, charming
- yellow – cheerful, energetic, lifts spirits, sunny, bright, hopeful, optimistic, joyful, clear, creates motion
- orange – denotes energy, warmth, sun, soothing, friendly, youthful, happy, motivated, garish
- red – empowering, stimulating, hot, exciting, attention-grabbing, powerful, passionate, loving, energetic
- teal – sophisticated, rich
- green – signifies growth, renewal, health, success, environment, balance, harmony, stability, money, and good luck

Definition

When we talk of useful arts in this section we mean things produced by craftsmen or artisans that are both beautiful and useful. The term "useful arts" can also apply to anything physical that is manufactured or produced, a much broader usage than we intend for this section.

This German ceramic plate has become a work of art.

Additional Layer

Medieval artisans were skilled professionals. They were either masters, who owned the company or they were journeymen or apprentices who worked for the masters.

Ancient Europe – Global Grids – Earth & Moon – Crafts

- purple – comforting, mysterious, creative, moody; represents royalty, passion, nobility, and spirituality
- blue – relaxing, cool, calming, peaceful, tranquil, harmonious, trusting, confident; represents water, truth, serenity, spaciousness, and comfort.

Now choose a setting – a restaurant, a corporate boardroom, a bedroom, a dining room, a kids' fort, anywhere. If you were in charge of choosing its look, what color would you choose? Use a dark piece of construction paper and some colored chalks. Dip the chalk for your color scheme into warm sugar water and then draw a simple design on the dark paper. You may want to compare several colors to sense the mood they portray. Wet chalk makes the colors vivid and particularly expressive.

☺ ☺ ☻ EXPLORATION: Homemade Wrapping Paper

Even the wrapping paper we buy has a utilitarian purpose, but the decorative elements of it are just as important. Make some of your own wrapping paper for a birthday or holiday. You can make stamps from sponges or potatoes, dip the stamps in paint and decorate plain newsprint or a brown paper bag for customized paper.

While you're at it, make some gift tags and bows to go along with your wrapping paper.

☺ ☺ EXPLORATION: Friendship Bracelets

This activity will especially appeal to girls. Jewelry is one art that never goes out of style with the ladies. And this is one that your girls will find beautiful and useful to wear or give to friends. (Boys will think it's cool if you use leather strips and make it as a key holder or pocket knife holder.)

You need to start with two or more colors of embroidery floss, which you can buy inexpensively at a craft store or in the craft section of a discount store. The only other thing you need is a safety pin.

1. Cut four strands of embroidery floss, 12 inches long each, in any colors you like.
2. Tie the strands of embroidery floss together in a knot at one end, leaving a tail long enough to tie the bracelet with later.

Additional Layer

Chefs are even concerned with the colors of foods. They try to make their dishes as beautiful as they are delicious. Do you think the appearance of it affects how people feel about the food they're eating?

Even door knobs and drawer pulls can be art.

Additional Layer

This lamp shade is a replica of a lamp designed by American artisan Louis Comfort Tiffany.

Photo by Hannes Grobbe

Ancient Europe – Global Grids – Earth & Moon – Crafts

3. Poke the safety pin through the knot and then pin it through the knee of your pants. This will hold it in place as you work.
4. Hold one strand in your right hand and the rest of the strands in your left. The strand in your right hand will make a right triangle and pass over the top of the other strands, then around the strands and through the triangle. (Here it is shown with just 2 strands. You can use multiple strands, but keep them together in a bunch as you pass the strand over and around the others.)

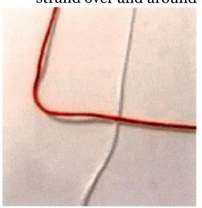 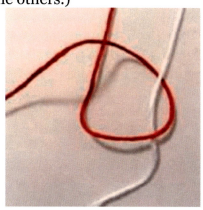

5. Pull the knot tight.
6. Now pick up the second strand and make a knot in the same way.
7. Continue making knots, one strand at a time until the bracelet is as long as you want it to be then tie off the other end.

Kids who get interested can learn many more, more complicated designs from a book or online.

☺ ☻ **EXPEDITION: Woodworking**
Major home improvement stores have clinics with free woodworking crafts for kids once a month, usually on Saturdays. Look for one near you.

Additional Layer

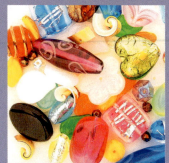

Besides friendship bracelets, beaded jewelry is another popular handmade art. We'll cover jewelry making more in Unit 1.17

Fabulous Fact
The art of friendship bracelets originated from the Native Americans. According to tradition, the friend who is the recipient of the bracelet must wear it until the cords wear out and it falls off on its own.

Additional Layer

Auditorium at the University of Technology, Helsinki, Finland, designed by famous architect Alvar Aalto

photo by J-P Karna

Ancient Europe – Global Grids – Earth & Moon – Crafts

Carving inside a church, Barcelona, Spain

Teaching Tip
There are digital scrapbooking programs you can purchase inexpensively if you want to easily design pages to print. They have lots of customizable templates and features and are really easy to use, even for kids.

Additional Layer
The same skills used for designing scrapbooks can be translated into other useful projects:

- creating marketing fliers (for their lawn mowing business perhaps?)
- making greeting cards
- creating an attractive science fair or history day display
- producing a yearbook, newspaper, or magazine layout

☻ ☻ **EXPLORATION: Build a Web Page**
There are so many free web site creators out there that your child can experiment with. Not only must web pages be useful, giving information people want, but they have to be eye catching too. We call this kind of art graphic art.

1. Start by signing up for a free blog from Blogger or Wordpress or a free site from Webs.com or another site creator. If you work with Blogger or Wordpress you ultimately have much more freedom of design than with a free site creator, and blogs can be kept private for just yourself or for only family and friends, a good idea for youthful creators.
2. If you've never worked with blog design, you can either jump right in and try to figure it out on your own, or you can check out a book from the library to guide you.
3. Use the site to keep a journal, post school work, or write about a topic near and dear.
4. As you post, you can keep working with and tweaking the design as you go.

Determined computer savvy kids may expand into learning HTML, the computer programming language.

☻ ☻ ☻ **EXPLORATION: Make a Scrapbook Page**
Scrapbooks are a useful way to colorfully and creatively display your photos in a book. You can use scrapbook papers and stickers from a craft store or you can create scrapbook pages on the computer using digital photos, clip art, and other designs.

To make a scrapbook page from craft store supplies:
1. Select 1 to 3 photos to use on your page. You don't want it too crowded.
2. Decide what the theme of your photos is: a day at the beach, sports photos, highlighting a person, etc.
3. Pick 2 to 3 colors you want to use on your page.
4. Go to the store, pick one sheet for the background, and stickers or other accessories in your companion colors to accent the page. Don't forget to stick with the few colors and theme you chose. Keep the design simple. Overly busy pages don't look as good as clean, neat pages.
5. Take your supplies home and lay out all your materials. Try out several different layouts before you glue or tape anything down.
6. Fasten all your photos, stickers and accessories to the page. Put your page into a sheet protector and insert into a three ring binder or photo binder made for the purpose.

Ancient Europe – Global Grids – Earth & Moon – Crafts

☺ ☺ ☻ EXPLORATION: Redecorate Your Room

Nathan chose white paint and dark blue trim for his walls.

Before you begin the actual decorating, you need to spend lots of time browsing through home decorating magazines, either in print and/or online. Look specifically for magazines or books directed toward kids' and teens' rooms. Start by making a scrapbook of what you like. If you see a room or a project that excites you, cut it out, paste it to a piece of paper, and pop it in your design notebook, a three ring notebook that you keep for design ideas. Write notes around the picture detailing what you like. Is it the colors? The furniture style? The window treatments?

Once you have made a collection of magazine pictures you can begin designing your own room. Color will probably be a big factor, but you may also notice that you really like clean modern lines or that you prefer dark wood furniture to painted furniture.

Tips for kids' bedrooms:
- Don't be afraid of color in a kid's room, but also don't paint something she'll love today and hate tomorrow. You want the more lasting things (like wall color and furniture) to be able to grow with them. Accessories are easy to change in and out.
- Consider what they own. When you design, you need to consider storage and usefulness. If a kid uses their room for homework, include a desk. If it's a friend hangout, plop beanbag chairs in there. Include enough storage so that everything can be put away in its

Elizabeth added removable vinyl lettering above her mirror. When she outgrows her princess room it will come right off.

Explanation

Each subject that you study has its own specific vocabulary words that go along with it. Artists, pilots, scientists – they all learn their own lingo. The best way to have a strong vocabulary across all disciplines is to read a lot.

But there are other things you can do. Latin is wonderful for learning English vocab since well over 50% of English words are derived from Latin or Greek. Many English words may be derived from a single Latin root. For example the word legis, meaning law, is in English words like legal, legislate, legitimate, and many more. If you know the root word legis, you can get a good idea of what even an unfamiliar word with that root means.

If you aren't interested in a whole Latin course, then I recommend taking a course focusing on just building vocab from Latin roots. I like *Vocabulary From Classical Roots* for junior high or high school.

Michelle

Ancient Europe – Global Grids – Earth & Moon – Crafts

place.
- Don't forget the details either. Making a pencil holder for your desk that coordinates with your bedspread can be the kind of touch that really makes you love your room.
- Cut the clutter. Get rid of the mismatched posters and sports photos, instead make conscious decisions about what kind of art or displays fit your personality.

When you are finished, take your own pictures. Before you start, look at a few catalogs or magazines that show rooms to get photography and staging ideas. Bring in extra lamps so the room is very bright – lighting is key. Second, kneel to take the picture. Magazine photos are always taken from a low angle; instead of looking down on the bed you should have the camera at the level of the bed. Try it and see. Finally take many different shots until you get just what you like.

Additional Layer

Like architecture and interior design, sewing is a useful art.

Tyler learning to sew a quiver for his toy arrows.

You may or may not have the desire to make your own clothing, toys, curtains, blankets, and other housewares. Regardless, sewing is definitely a useful skill to have. Sewing on a button or doing some hand embroidery is a great start. Most communities also offer basic sewing classes as well.

Coming up next . . .

Unit 1-4
Ancient Greece
Wonders of the World
Satellites - Greek Art

Ancient Europe – Global Grids – Earth & Moon – Crafts

My Ideas For This Unit:

Title: _____ Topic: _____

_____
_____
_____
_____
_____
_____
_____
_____
_____

Title: _____ Topic: _____

_____
_____
_____
_____
_____
_____
_____
_____
_____

Title: _____ Topic: _____

_____
_____
_____
_____
_____
_____
_____
_____
_____

Ancient Europe – Global Grids – Earth & Moon – Crafts

My Ideas For This Unit:

Title: _____ Topic: _____

_____
_____
_____
_____
_____
_____
_____
_____

Title: _____ Topic: _____

_____
_____
_____
_____
_____
_____
_____
_____

Title: _____ Topic: _____

_____
_____
_____
_____
_____
_____
_____
_____

Stonehenge

Stonehenge is an ancient and mysterious rock sculpture in England. We aren't sure exactly who built it, why they built it, or how they got those huge rocks from far away and stacked them in formation. It could be a temple for worship, a place of healing, a huge calendar, a burial site, or something else entirely.

Ancient Europe: Unit 1-3

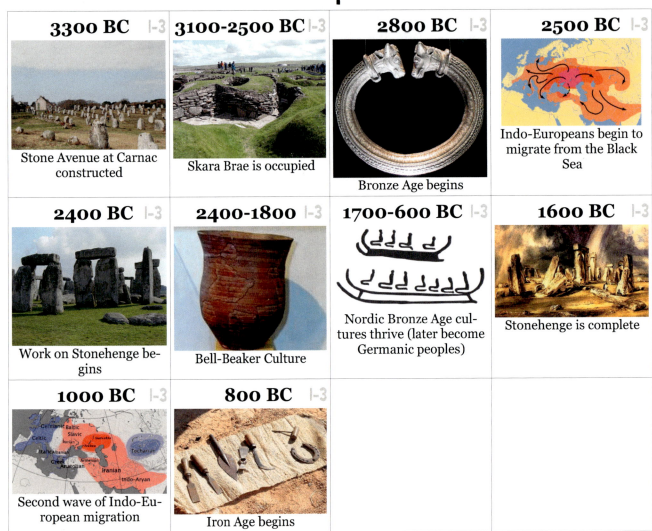

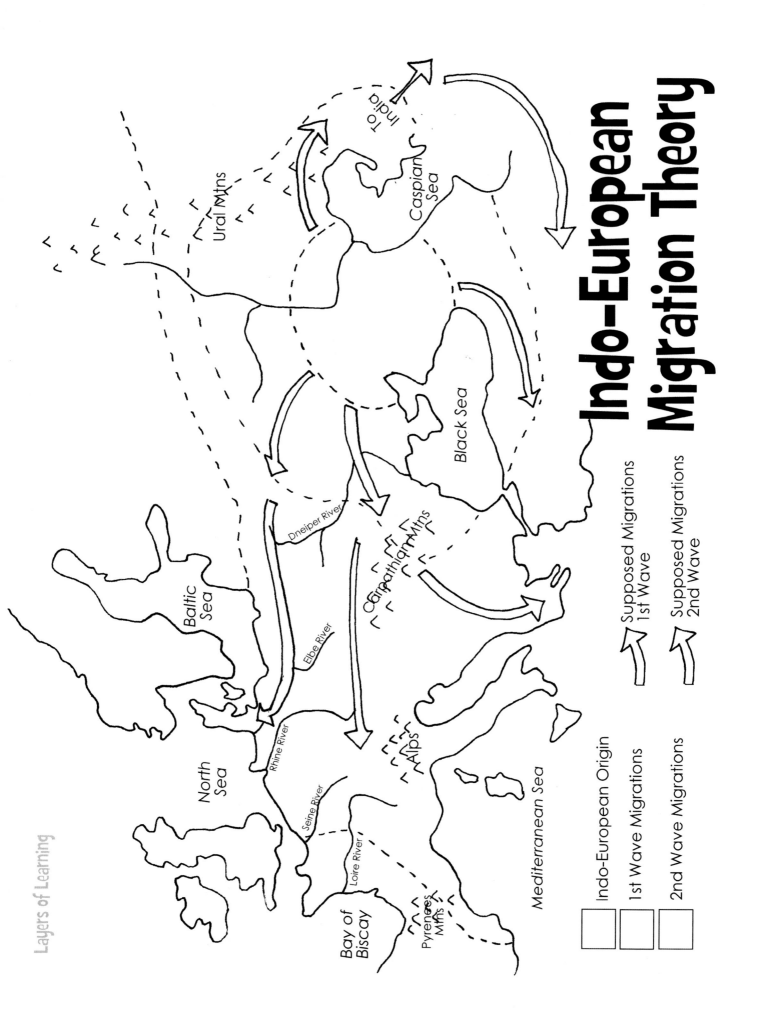

Bell-Beaker People

■ Bell-Beaker Cultural Areas

Cattle and Sheep

Archery

Bell-Beaker Pottery

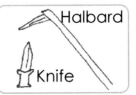
Halbard
Knife

Megalithic Sites

Copper Ore Smelting

Color the areas of the Bell-Beaker Culture.

Cut out the pictures to the left. Paste them to the map in the spaces provided. The order doesn't matter.

Layers of Learning

World Map

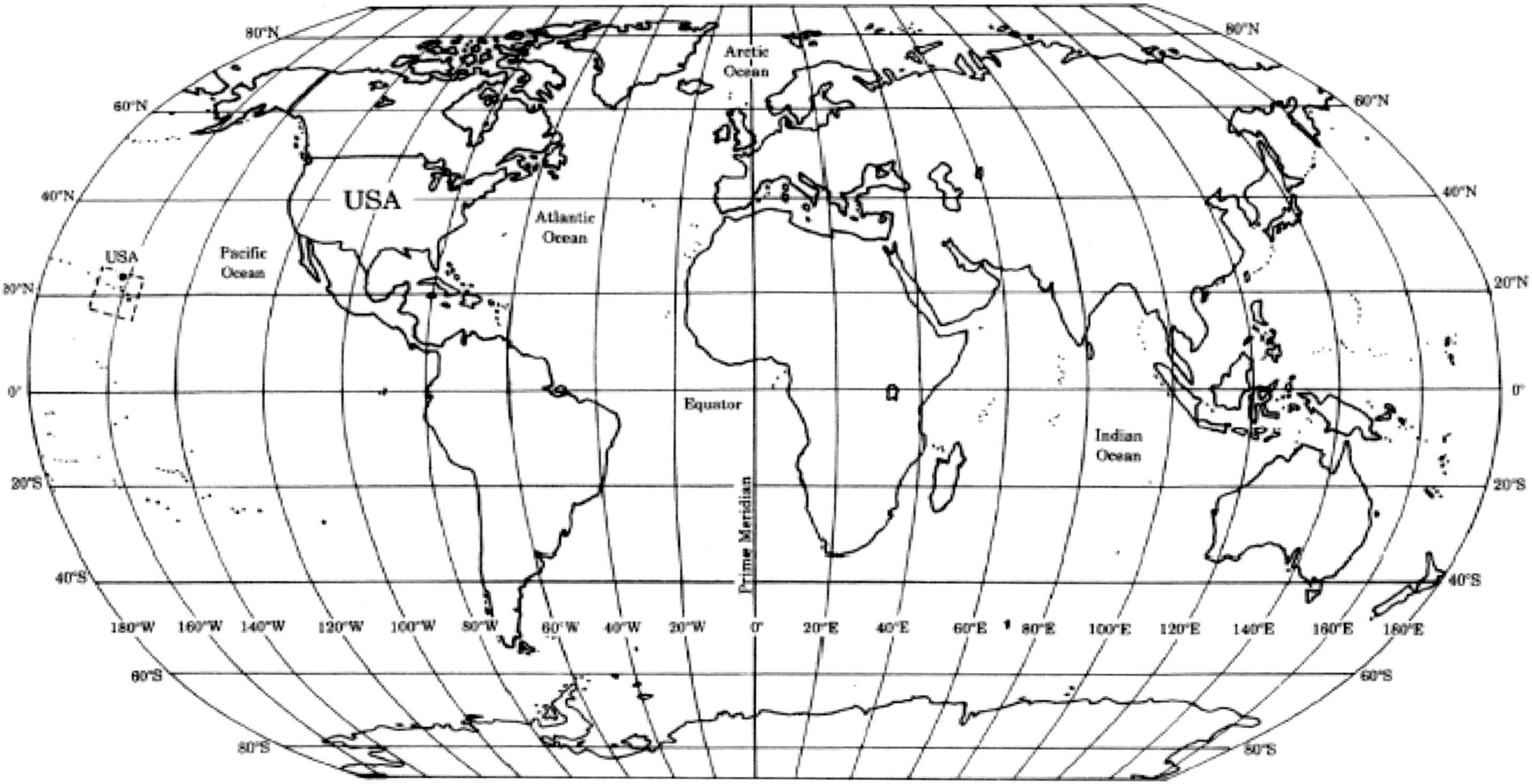

Pacific Ocean

USA

Atlantic Ocean

Arctic Ocean

Prime Meridian

Equator

Indian Ocean

180°W, 160°W, 140°W, 120°W, 100°W, 80°W, 60°W, 40°W, 20°W, 0°, 20°E, 40°E, 60°E, 80°E, 100°E, 120°E, 140°E, 160°E, 180°E

80°N, 60°N, 40°N, 20°N, 0°, 20°S, 40°S, 60°S, 80°S

www.layers-of-learning.com

Earth, Moon, & Stars Mobile

Copy these on to card stock. Cut them out, decorate them, and hang them from a wire using string to create a mobile.

Layers of Learning

About the Authors

Karen & Michelle . . .
Mothers, sisters, teachers, women who are passionate
about educating kids.
We are dedicated to lifelong learning.

Karen, a mother of four, who has homeschooled her kids for more than eight years with her husband, Bob, has a bachelor's degree in child development with an emphasis in education. She lives in Utah where she gardens, teaches piano, and plays an excruciating number of board games with her kids. Karen is our resident Arts expert and English guru {most necessary as Michelle regularly and carelessly mangles the English language and occasionally steps over the bounds of polite society}.

Michelle and her husband, Cameron, homeschooling now for over a decade, teach their six boys on their ten acres in beautiful Idaho country. Michelle earned a bachelors in biology, making her the resident Science expert, though she is mocked by her friends for being the *Botanist with the Black Thumb of Death*. She also is the go-to for History and Government. She believes in staying up late, hot chocolate, and a no whining policy. We both pitch in on Geography, in case you were wondering, and are on a continual quest for knowledge.

*Visit our constantly updated blog for tons of free ideas,
free printables, and more cool stuff for sale:
www.Layers-of-Learning.com*

Made in the USA
Monee, IL
07 August 2020